101 SIGNS of DESIGN

one hundred one

of

TIMELESS TRUTHS FROM THE WORD

one hundred one 101 SIGNS of DESIGN

TIMELESS TRUTHS FROM THE WORD
HENRY M. MORRIS

Master Books

First printing: August 2002

ISBN: 0-89051-366-X
Library of Congress Catalog Card Number: 2002105382

Printed in the United States of America.
Please visit our website for other great titles:
www.masterbooks.net
For information regarding author interviews, please
contact the publicity department at (870) 438-5288.

one hundred one SIGNS of DESIGN

INTRODUCTION

The 101 quotations in this little book are, of course, taken from various books written by me, Dr. Henry M. Morris, and selected by Jim Fletcher, editor, in support of the biblical doctrine of creation. However, it is the Bible itself that gives relevance to anything I, he, or anyone else could ever write on this subject.

Surely anyone who has read the Bible carefully will know that there is no hint there whatsoever of evolution or the alleged long ages that supposedly could have allowed time for evolution. For example, God himself wrote the following claim, penned on the stone tablets of the Ten Commandments: For in six days the LORD made heaven and earth, the sea, and all that in them is, and rested the seventh day (Exod. 20:11).

This verse is said actually to have been written directly by "the finger of God" (Deut. 9:10). That is, all of the Bible is divinely inspired, but this particular fact was divinely *inscribed*. The context of Exodus 20:8–11 precludes any meaning for these "days" except that of literal 24-hour time periods.

Furthermore, these six days all occurred relatively recently, just several thousand years ago. Jesus said, "But from the beginning of the creation God made them male and female" (Mark 10:6), quoting the account of Adam and Eve's creation in Genesis 1:27. Note: *not* billions of years *after* the beginning!

Jesus Christ was there, so He would know! There was no time for evolution, and there is no evidence, neither biblical

nor scientific, for true macroevolution. The Lord Jesus "finished" the creation in the beginning, then several thousand years later "finished" His wonderful gift of salvation for all who believe on Him (Gen. 2:1–3; John 19:30).

May the quotations presented here be a testament to the Creator and His Word, and may each one who reads come away with a deeper sense of awe and respect for Him.

We are living today in what many are calling a post-modern age — an age when there are no absolutes and almost anything goes. A more realistic designation, however, might be the post-Christian age, when almost any kind of belief and practice except biblical Christianity is tolerated and even encouraged.

One world view is expressed in terms of evolution and the other one by divine creation. . . . We must believe in either one world view or the other; we cannot really believe both because each is the opposite of the other. One is God-centered; the other is creature-centered.

There is no doubt ... that the Lord Jesus Christ believed and taught the absolute verbal inerrancy of all the Bible. Therefore, we who believe Him and seek to follow Him must do the same.

4

He said that
"the scripture cannot be broken"
(John 10:35). Evolutionists may try to break it; New Agers and

occultists may try to break it; secularists and hedonists may try to

break it; all manner of skeptics and doubters and even compromising

Christians may try to break it. But the Scripture cannot be broken!

The fact is that no dilution of the creation/flood record of God's inspired Word, no matter how well motivated and persuasively written, is going to budge the evolutionary establishment in science or education one iota. They hold their position for religious reasons, not scientific.

The first law (law of energy conservation)
tells us that no energy is now being created, so the universe could
not have created itself. The only scientific conclusion is that "In the beginning God created the heavens and the earth" (Gen. 1:1).

The gospel is connected with creation because *Jesus Christ himself is the Creator.*

8

In a very real sense, *Christianity is Christ*,

so that defending the Christian faith must focus

especially on the person and work of Christ.

Special creation is a concept found only in the Bible. To the ancient Israelites, accustomed as they were to thinking in terms of the evolutionary cosmologies of the Egyptians and the Canaanites, this was a radically new idea.

The special creation of our space-mass-time universe is declared in the introductory statement of the Word of God: "In the beginning [time] God created the heaven [space] and the earth [mass]" (Gen. 1:1).

Skeptics sometimes attempt to ridicule the biblical chronology by saying, "But if the creation took place only 6,000 years ago, what was God doing before that?" One can surely see, however, that this is the same question as "What was God doing prior to the hypothetical creation of the universe five billion years ago?" Infinity minus 6,000 is exactly the same as infinity minus 5 billion.

12

Although creation is the foundation, it is not the entire structure, and it is sad that many who believe in creation are still unsaved, because they "obey not the gospel of our Lord Jesus Christ" (2 Thess. 1:8).

If God had meant to convey the idea of long ages, He could easily have used a number of other Hebrew words and phrases to convey that idea. All the ancients were already familiar with the concept of long ages of evolutionary change in their various nature religions.

Furthermore, *the order of events in Genesis* flagrantly contradicts the order assigned by evolutionary astronomers and geologists in well over a dozen ways.

Although there are many, many references to creation throughout the Bible, *there is no hint anywhere* of long ages before man's creation.

16

If the gap theory were valid, it would mean that God had instituted an ages-long system of suffering and death over the world, before there were ever any men and women to place in dominion over that world, and then suddenly destroy it in a violent cataclysm. Why would an omnipotent, merciful God do such a wasteful and cruel thing as that?

But if "death reigned," not "from Adam to Moses" as the Bible says (Rom. 5:14), but had already reigned for billions of years before Adam, then death is not the wages of sin but instead was part of God's creative purpose. *How then could the death of Christ put away sin?*

The gap theory has no scientific merit, requires a very forced biblical exegesis, and leads to a God-dishonoring theology. It does not work, neither biblically nor scientifically.

By stretching the six days of creation into great ages, many evolutionists can put up with the Genesis "story" of creation, but they simply cannot tolerate the record of man's Fall and God's curse as the cause of suffering and death in the world.

20

The great fossil graveyard in the earth's crust all over the world cannot be a record of the progressive creation of life over many long ages, but must actually be a record of the worldwide destruction of life in one age . . . at the time of the great Flood.

A world of pain, cruelty, suffering, and death

is the result of man's sin, not of God's love.

It is arrogant for a hell-bound sinner to impose conditions upon God's offer of salvation, presuming to tell God which parts of His Word he will believe and obey before he does God the favor of accepting His offer of salvation.

It is obvious that, despite loud protests, evolution does not fit the traditional definition of science at all. That is, *no one has ever observed evolution happening,* and the essence of the scientific method is experimentation and observation.

There have been great numbers of extinctions

during the period of human history, but

no documented originations.

If one probes deeply enough, he will usually find that people believe in evolution either because of passive acceptance of majority opinion or else because of emotional antipathy to biblical Christianity — not because of scientific evidence.

The main reason for insisting on the universal flood as a fact of history and as the primary vehicle for geological interpretation is that *God's Word plainly teaches it!* No geologic difficulties, real or imagined, can be allowed to take precedence over the clear statements and necessary inferences of Scripture.

It is precisely because biblical revelation is absolutely authoritative and perspicuous that the scientific facts, rightly interpreted, will give the same testimony as that of Scripture. There is not the slightest possibility that the "facts" of science can contradict the Bible.

28

The summary of Genesis 2:1–3 says that "all the host" of things God "created and made" was "finished" after the six days, and that God stopped any further work of creation or development. Modern geologists and biologists say that the same processes used to bring the world to its present form are still in operation, and "creation" is still continuing.

Evolution is a wasteful, inefficient, and cruel process. Surely an omnipotent God could devise a better plan than this. Most importantly, a God of love and grace could never be guilty of imposing such a monstrously sadistic system on His living creatures.

Whenever "vertical changes" do occur, they are never upward toward higher levels of organization; they are always downward — imperfections, mutations, death, sometimes even extinction — exactly the reverse of what true evolution should require.

The fossil record reveals the same types of phenomena as the living world; that is, horizontal changes within limits and unbridged gaps between the basic kinds. Although many fossilized animals are now extinct, out of the billions of fossils *there are no true transitional forms*.

32

It seems as certain as science can be certain, that the basic laws of nature are not in a process of continuing evolution, but rather of conservation and stability, exactly as predicted by the creation model!

There is no way to control mutations to make them produce characteristics which might be needed. Natural selection must simply take what comes.

That the net effect of mutations is harmful, rather than beneficial, to the supposed progress of evolution, is made transparently clear by the zeal with which evolutionists for decades have been trying to get mutation-producing radiations removed from the environment!

It is significant that *not one new species* of plant or animal is known to have evolved on earth during recorded history, but large numbers have become extinct.

36

Practically all the so-called "vestigial" organs, *especially those in man, have been proved in recent years to have definite uses and not to be vestigial at all.*

Present–day geologic processes, acting at the same rates as at present, cannot possibly account for the geologic events of the past.

The present is not the key to the past!

The evolution model, of course, demands an immensity of time. . . . Not even thirty billion years would suffice for the chance evolution of even the simplest living molecule, but somehow evolutionists continue to believe in evolution anyway.

40

Evolution is not merely a biological theory of little significance. It is a world view — the world view diametrically opposing the Christian world view.

The standard system says insects came before birds, but the Bible says the "creeping things" (defined as insects in Lev. 11) were made on the sixth day and birds on the fifth day.

All the hard data in the life sciences show that evolution is not occurring today, all the real data in the earth sciences show it did not occur in the past, and all the genuine data in the physical sciences show it is not possible at all. Nevertheless, evolution is almost universally accepted as a fact in all the natural sciences.

Evolution is the cruelest, most wasteful, and most irrational method of "creation" that could ever be imagined, not even to mention the fact that it *is scientifically untenable*.

44

Man was originally a vegetarian according to Scripture (Gen. 1:29); anthropologists maintain that the earliest men were not only hunters and meat eaters, but probably cannibals.

Darwin's idea that evolution means "the preservation of favored races in the struggle for life" eventually led to Nazism and the Jewish holocaust — even though Darwin himself would have been appalled at the thought.

Evolution dominates not only all disciplines of modern thought, but all modern political systems and philosophies as well.

Evolution is *not a modern scientific theory* at all, but only the ancient rebellion of men against their Creator.

48

It is not too much to say that there is *literally no scientific evidence* whatever — past, present, or future — for any real evolution. Belief in evolution is strictly a matter of faith.

Evolution and creation are on the same ground. Both must be seen with the eye of faith, because neither can be seen taking place with our physical eyes. But this very fact is **a strong argument for creation** *and against evolution.*

The point is that, out of the many billions of fossils known to be preserved in the sedimentary rocks of the earth's crust, including representatives of many still-living types of plants and animals, no true transitional fossil forms have yet been discovered!

Thus, *there are no transitional forms* leading up to the mammals. Furthermore, each of the 32 orders of mammals (rodents, insectivores, ungulates, primates, etc.) is drastically different from all others, with no intermediates!

Anthropologists are like the blind men looking at
the elephant, each sampling only a small part of the total reality.

Neanderthal Man and Cro-Magnon Man are *now universally accepted as* Homo sapiens. *Even* Ramapithecus *is currently out of favor as an early hominid, being recognized now as simply an orangutan.*

Piltdown Man was a hoax, Peking Man has been lost for 50 years, and Java Man was later admitted by its discoverer to be an artificial construct of a human thighbone and the skull of a gibbon. Other former "stars" in the ape-man extravaganza were Nebraska Man (an extinct pig) and Neanderthal Man (now universally acknowledged to be modern man).

That the australopithecines were simple apes of some kind is evident also from their skulls, which have long been recognized as having the brain capacity of a true ape. It was long believed, however, that their brains were at least probably human-like in shape. This now also turns out to have been quite wrong.

56

Since we can never observe evolution
in action, it is presumed to happen very rapidly when
we are not looking. No wonder it has been so
hard to learn how evolution works!

The only alternative [to evolution] *seems to be creationism, and that, to the leaders of evolutionary thought, is unthinkable heresy. So, instead of turning to God, they attribute the generation of each new kind of organism to some mysterious genetic upheaval, some remarkable embryonic saltation, some lucky leap of jumping genes, transforming a decadent population of organisms in equilibrium, to a new and higher degree of biologic existence!*

The evolutionist has long used mutations as his explanation of the origin of new features in organisms. The main problem has been that real mutations always turn out to be harmful.

Consequently, *if one will not accept creation,* he simply has to believe in some as-yet-undiscovered mechanism that will cause new and more complex organisms to evolve all at once — or at least so rapidly as to leave no record of the few intermediate steps.

60

Real evolutionists are committed religiously to
evolutionism, and they will continue to believe in it, or at least to
promulgate it, no matter what the evidence shows against it.

One of the most famous of the living fossils has been the coelacanth fish, which supposedly became extinct in the Cretaceous period about 70 million years ago, but which suddenly turned up still alive and well in the Indian Ocean near Madagascar.

The flying insects are especially noteworthy. Their wings are not like the wings of birds, bats, or flying reptiles. Each type of wing is supposed by evolutionists to have evolved independently of the others. *(Seriously, what are the "chances" of this?)*

The Bible stresses ten times that the entities created were to reproduce "after their kinds." Evolutionists postulate the slow ascent of all organisms from a common ancestor.

64

In the Bible, Adam gave names to all the land animals God had formed. Geologists claim that most of them were extinct long before man was on the earth.

The evolutionist maintains that the first marine life was a minute blob of complex chemicals, **but the Bible says** *that God caused an abundance of marine life (Gen. 1:20–21) in great variety when He first created it.*

God told men to exercise dominion over every organism He had created on the previous days (Gen. 1:28). According to the geologic-age system, the vast majority of such organisms were already extinct for ages before man appeared.

Why would [an omnipotent Creator] have to "create" something by a slow, wasteful, cruel process requiring millions of years? It would be far more reasonable for Him to **create every system in His universe** *fully mature and functioning in its intended purpose right from the start.*

68   *To explain a* discrepancy between 1 million and 2,000 years, for the time from the first man to the time of Abraham (about 2,000 B.C. by secular chronology) in terms of genealogical gaps means that the average such gap between each pair of names in Genesis 5 and 11 is more than 50,000 years! Each "gap" is therefore more than eight times as long as the entire period of recorded history.

God's work of creation . . . was that of calling into existence out of nothing that which had no existence in any form before. Only God can create in this sense, and in all the Bible, no other subject appears for the verb "create" than God.

The account of creation in Genesis 1 indicates that at least ten major categories of organic life were specially created, each *"after his kind."* . . . Even though there may be uncertainty as to what is meant by "kind," it is obvious that the word does have a definite and fixed meaning. One "kind" could not transform itself into another "kind."

Evolution is inconsistent with God's omnipotence. Since *He has all power, He is capable of creating* the universe in an instant, rather than having to stretch out His creating over eons of time.

72

Evolution is inconsistent with God's personality. If man in His own image was the goal of the evolutionary process, surely God should not have waited until the very tail end of geologic time before creating personalities. No personal fellowship was possible with the rocks and seas, or even with the dinosaur and gliptodons.

Evolution is inconsistent with God's omniscience. The history of evolution, as interpreted by evolutionary geologists from the fossil record, is filled with extinctions, misfits, evolutionary cul-de-sacs, and other like evidences of very poor planning. The very essence of evolution, in fact, is random mutation, not scientific progress.

Evolution is inconsistent with *God's nature of love.* The supposed fact of evolution is best evinced by the fossils, which eloquently speak of a harsh world, filled with storm and upheaval, disease and famine, struggle for existence, and violent death. The accepted mechanism for inducing evolution is overpopulation and a natural selection through extermination of the weak and unfit. A loving God would surely have been more considerate of His creatures than this.

Evolution is inconsistent with God's purposiveness. *If God's purpose was the creation and redemption of man, as theistic evolutionists presumably believe, it seems incomprehensible that He would waste billions of years in aimless evolutionary meandering before getting to the point. What semblance of purpose could there have been in the hundred-million-year reign and eventual extinction of the dinosaurs, for example?*

76   *Evolution is inconsistent with* **the grace of God.**
Evolution, with its theology of struggle for survival in the physical
world, fits perfectly with the humanistic theory of works for
salvation in the spiritual world. The Christian concept of the grace of
God, providing life and salvation in response to faith alone on the
basis of the willing sacrifice of himself for the unfit and unworthy, is
diametrically opposite to the evolutionary concept.

The writer of Genesis 1 clearly intended to describe a creation accomplished in six literal days. He could not possibly have expressed such a meaning any more clearly and emphatically than in the words and sentences which are actually used.

The familiar verse 2 Peter 3:8, "One day is with the Lord as a thousand years," has been badly misapplied when used to teach the day-age theory. . . . Peter is dealing here with the conflict between uniformitarianism and creationism prophesied in the last days. His is saying that, despite man's naturalistic scoffings, *God can do in one day what,* on uniformitarian premises, *might seem to require a thousand years.*

But if the rocks of the earth's crust were already filled with fossilized remains of billions of animals, and even of hominid forms that looked like men, then God himself is directly responsible for creating suffering and death, not in judgment upon rebellion, but as an integral factor of His work of creation and sovereign rule. And this is theological chaos!

80

Catastrophism does provide the key to the geological ages, not an imagined cataclysm before Genesis 1:2 that supposedly allows us to retain the geological age system, but, rather, the very real Noachian cataclysm which destroys it.

If the Bible is the Word of God — *and it is* — and if Jesus Christ is the infallible and omniscient Creator — *and He is* — then it must be firmly believed that the world and all things in it were created in six natural days, and that the long geological ages of evolutionary history never really took place at all.

According to Genesis, plants appeared on the third day, and insects only on the sixth. This would be impossible if the days were ages, since plants require insect pollination for their continued survival.

If the mountains were the same elevation then as now, as the local-flood theory would imply, the waters were at least 17,000 feet high (Mt. Ararat, on which the ark rested, reaches this altitude) for a period of at least nine months. To require such a condition to be a "local" flood imposes impossible hydraulic demands on the water involved. One has to assume a sort of egg-shaped flood three miles high!

84   *The ark had* a carrying capacity at least equal to that of 522 standard railroad stock cars, as can be quickly calculated from its recorded dimensions (Gen. 6:15). This is more than twice as large as necessary to accommodate two of every species of known land animal that ever lived. If the Flood were only a local or regional flood, it would be folly to spend 120 years to prepare an ark large enough to carry animals from the whole world. Its size was absurdly out of proportion for a mere regional fauna.

Moreover, the . . . animals (as well as humans) could easily have escaped a local flood by the obvious expedient of migrating to higher ground elsewhere.

God's unequivocal promise never again to send the Flood (Gen. 9:11) has been broken repeatedly if the Noachian flood were only a local flood.

The Lord Jesus Christ himself, as well as
Peter (2 Pet. 2:5; 3:6) and the author of Hebrews (Heb. 11:7),
confirmed that the Flood at least destroyed all mankind. Christ said,
"The flood came, and destroyed them all" (Luke 17:27).

88

The entire biblical doctrine of substitution and
blood redemption becomes meaningless if death and bloodshed
reigned in the world for ages before sin came into the world.

When the Pharisees asked [Christ] about marriage and divorce, He replied that "from the beginning of the creation God made them male and female" (Mark 10:6). He did not say that God made the first man and woman 15 billion years after *the beginning of the creation,* but right from *the beginning of the creation.*

Jesus called Satan "a liar and the father of it," as well as "a murderer from the beginning" (John 8:44). He had not only deceived Eve with his humanistic philosophy: "Ye shall be as gods" (Gen. 3:5), but also he had caused Cain to murder God's first prophet, his brother Abel. This, too, was at "the beginning," not five billion years after the beginning, for even if animals had been dying for a billion years before this, as theistic evolutionists assert, their deaths could not be called "murders."

If animals have been living and dying on the earth for millions of years before man was created, the very concept of human dominion over them becomes essentially trivial, if not ridiculous. What would be the point of man's exercising stewardship over the animals for a few thousand years when they had gotten along very well without him for a hundred million years!

92

Creation is not a peripheral doctrine. In fact,
*biblical creationism is the most important
of all biblical teachings,* because it is the very
foundation of everything else in the Bible.

"In the beginning God created the heaven and the earth."

These opening words of the Bible constitute what is at once *the most simple and the most profound statement ever made.* This is the most widely known sentence ever written, easily understood by the simplest child, yet inexhaustibly compatible with the most advanced scientific comprehension of the universe.

[The first verse of Genesis] *is the first and only statement of real creation* in all the cosmogonies of all the nations of past or present. All other creation myths begin with the universe already in existence, in watery chaos or in some other primordial form. Evidently man, with unaided reason, cannot conceive of true creation; he must begin with something.

Each verse in the [creation] account began with
the conjunction of sequence — "and" (Hebrew waw). There
was no suggestion of allegory, overlap, gap, or of anything
except straightforward history. The conjunction "and,"
indicating chronological sequence, actually was used
some 60 times in the creation narrative.

Einstein felt that the most incredible thing about the universe was that it is intelligible, capable of being described in ways intelligible to men and women. How could random, non-intelligent primeval particles evolve themselves into orderly, intelligible systems?

The world is a cosmos, not a chaos.

Geologists say that the earth's waters gradually oozed out of its interior over long ages. *Genesis says that the earth was covered* with water right from the beginning (Gen. 1:2).

Geologists say life originated in the primeval oceans.
*Genesis 1:11 says the first life
was on the land.*

Evolutionary geology teaches that the sun and moon are at least as old as the earth, whereas Genesis 1:14–19 says they were made **right in the middle of the period of creation,** *on the fourth day.*

Genesis says that plant life, even in such an advanced form as the fruit tree, was made one "day" before the sun and stars, but this would have been impossible if the day were really an aeon, since plants must have sunlight.

Books by Henry Morris
and published by Master Books, Green Forest, Arkansas

The Beginning of the World (1977).
The Bible Has the Answer, with Martin E. Clark (1987).
The Biblical Basis for Modern Science (2002).
Biblical Creationism (2000).
Christian Education for the Real World (1977).
Creation and the Second Coming (1991).
Defending the Faith (1999).
The God Who Is Real (2000).
The Long War Against God (2000).
Many Infallible Proofs, with Henry M. Morris III (1974).

Men of Science, Men of God (1982).
The Modern Creation Trilogy, with John D. Morris (1996).
The Remarkable Record of Job (2000).
The Remarkable Wisdom of Solomon (2001).
Scientific Creationism (1974).
That Their Words May Be Used Against Them (1997).
Treasures in the Psalms (2000).
What Is Creation Science? with Gary Parker (1982).
When Christians Roamed the Earth, with various other authors (2001).

Henry Morris

Dr. Henry Morris, with his copious writings about the creation/evolution debate, has earned the title "The Father of Modern Creationism." He is a respected scientist as well, and has written a number of textbooks in his own scientific field. He is the founder and now president emeritus of the Institute for Creation Research. He lives in California.